Selling to the Worst Customers

Introduction

I must admit, I have been a worst customer. By "worst", I don't necessarily being rude or demanding a lower price. This certainly happens, and I would imagine you would know first hand. Otherwise, you probably would be reading something else.

I am not proud of my attitude in the past. I learned some things the hard way when buying (or trying to buy) things in the past. Aside from being an immature brat (and let's be honest, who hasn't been?), a lot of this had to do with not knowing how to properly spend what income I had, so I was looking for cheap instead of value.

In my previous book *Stop Thinking in Reverse,* I discuss how to effectively handle your finances, no matter how much you make (or don't). The method I describe is what helped me to manage my money, become a better customer and also become better person. When used properly, it can completely change the trajectory of your financial future.

Selling and Success

It has been said that to be successful, find the job no one else wants to do. I personally believe that job to be sales. Whether retail, business-to-business, online or anywhere, sales drives the economy. This is how you hear about someone making a fortune and someone else went broke during a recession.

The job of selling itself is abhorrent to some people. I was one of them. I used to say "I am not a salesman." Well, I still believe that much to be true. I am also an author, recording artist and many other things.

What I was really saying back then was that I didn't believe I was cut out for it. I did eventually at the caveat, "maybe I haven't found the right thing to sell yet."

The latter could be the key for some people, even if they are already in sales. It is certainly possible to learn the product or service and present it to a customer. It's something different to be completely sold on the product yourself.

Interestingly, you may already be sold on that product or service. That may come as a surprise, but think about it. If you have been worked at a company many years, if you chose a college major, if you run a small business, if you're an author, a musician or if you simply have a goal you are determined to achieve, you're already sold!

That doesn't mean you'll necessarily work in a sales position, but it does mean that you've committed to a passion or conviction. If you're passionate about something, you want to tell everyone!

"Sales is nothing more than a transfer of feeling." - Zig Ziglar

The great Zig Ziglar wasn't being naive, however. He acknowledges the need for rest and balance in daily life. One especially important point he makes in *How to Be a Winner* is to recognize when you're down (i.e. sad, sick or injured, tragedy, emergency, etc.). However, when you are down, you must decide how long you will be down and when you will get back up. Then you get back up.

Whether you press too hard or don't press at all, you will reach a breaking point. I've been at both extremes more times than I can count. It was becoming a pattern and I had to interrupt it.

"I am not afraid of a person who knows 10000 kicks. But I am afraid of a person who knows one kick but practices it for 10000 times." - Bruce Lee

Someone practicing any skill to that extent has seen its efficacy or lack thereof in nearly any situation. If it doesn't work one way, it will in another, but there is something else to consider within this concept.

I personally believe if you play to your strengths, then the weaknesses start to catch up. I think Lee is implying this, although the quote itself is addressing the importance of specializing in something.

Specializing in a profession is an example of being sold on an idea. If it is a passion, the specialist will generally perform better than someone who is not passionate about it. The latter is possibly sold on something else (money, status, etc.).

Sales is about making money, and that's why some people will either avoid it or misuse it. However, this behavior means they missed the point or more likely, were never really told.

In order to properly sell, there is a common factor. The same goes for any profession, business practice, government, educational institution, and every individual. That last word. The individual. People.

People make money. Without people, there is no business. Treat them poorly, they go somewhere else. Treat them well, they keep coming back.

Even if you never work in sales, I highly recommend studying it. You'll be surprised what you'll discover about psychology, human relations, communication and more. When I first decided to learn about it, one of my main reasons was (and it's somewhat embarrassing to admit this) to have an advantage over salespeople.

I didn't want to get scammed. No one does. I actually did learn some tactics and was able to pick out certain methods when I encountered them.

"The first one to become belligerent loses." - Grant Cardone

RED FLAG!

Here are some red flags to be aware of:

"Can you really put a price on (insert product/service/idea here)?"

First of all, the seller has put a price on it, so this literally insults a buyer's intelligence. Even if the customer needs the item, they were probably better off buying elsewhere. I have walked out on a salesperson acting this way, and you should, too. That company doesn't deserve your business.

High pressure

The previous question could be considered high pressure, but it is worth considering the seller may actually be trying to help, albeit misguided. However, resorting to high pressure is never a good idea.

"Convince a man against his will, He's of the same opinion still." - Mary Wollstonecraft

Anything that induces a negative emotion in order to move a customer to buy might be akin to coercion. This is annoying at best and bullying at worse. There's a good chance anyone using these tactics is already under pressure from their boss.

There are differing opinions on this, and depending on how you're selling, there may be a legitimate time to introduce or navigate some negative emotion.

One example would be someone going to a mechanic because their car's brakes are grinding. That is a major safety concern, and if the mechanic doesn't mention that, it would be unethical. The context makes the difference.

Arrogance, interrupting, inflexibility and anything else that you don't want done to you has no place in business, regardless of what anyone told you. This is simply transferring the wrong emotion, and people don't forget how a person made them feel.

Unwillingness to negotiate

There are exceptions, of course, as not all sales can be negotiated on (retail pricing, service fees, recurring charges, etc.). However, even within those business models, there are opportunities for discounts and promotions.

Negotiation is sales, even if there is no monetary transaction. I've noticed that in many businesses, employees avoid actually talking to customers. I get it. I didn't want to.

There's a clear difference in not knowing what you're doing and knowing what to do and not doing it. If an employee isn't at least visible and available to answer my questions, I will find another place.

As far as a company is able, negotiation with customers should be an option. The most common complaint is price.

Are there payment plans? Are they even looking at the right product for their needs? Do you not have what they require? Did you listen to what they had to say?

None of those have anything to do with lowering the price, but all are forms of negotiation. Even if you don't make the sale, a simple conversation relevant to the product or service is quite refreshing for a customer. You can be friendly and professional, and it doesn't have to be a chore. If it is, you need to study sales, and I'll tell you why.

Regarding what I mentioned earlier, sales will teach you more about human behavior than you can learn in a psychology course. Psychology as a study is based on observations of things that already happened. Sales are what does happen. Do you understand the difference?

You can learn about it or practice it, and sales is practicing. Even if you never intend to sell anything, the insight will help more than you may realize. After awhile, you'll start to see how it works in the real world. The best part is, you'll learn skills that few people have and you'll have an advantage in any social setting, relationship or business. Use it wisely.

It was (and always will be) sales that drives the future, and it's not because of money. People had to be sold on the idea of the horseless carriage, the talking picture, the portable telephone, even literacy. All of these involved an idea before a product, and they all required a person before a dollar.

Academic Pursuit

Working in sales (and extensive research on the topic) made me realize that the product or service is worth what the buyer will pay for. You may have heard that before.

So that begs the question, who is a buyer? First off, they're not a buyer until they (surprise!) buy something. Until that point, they are a customer or prospect.

Let's take into consideration for a moment that money itself is essentially worthless. What this means is that money is simply what we agree it is. For our purposes, we need to recognize that money is simply a medium of exchange. In practice, money has no value until it is used. Numbers and figures won't make sense until an exchange (i.e. a transfer of funds) is made.

Again, sales is not just about making money. It's definitely there, but people are the deciding factor. You will meet (and probably have already) people with varying financial means.

Your role as a salesperson is to treat a person with a low income as well as you would a billionaire. No one ever found success by eliminating a certain group of people entirely.

That's certainly debatable, because many industries and companies will default to a qualified buyer. There is a reason for this. You have to sell where the money is. Keep in mind, however, even the non-qualified buyers sometimes will become qualified.

One way to address this is providing different products for different budgets. For example, a luxury car may sell for $100,000, but another brand owned by the parent company may sell a car for $30000, making a product more affordable to many other customers. That demand is there, obviously. Selling only to a single, qualified buyer is not ideal for most companies.

This is even more obvious in low or moderate priced goods. Fast food restaurants sell different sized drinks, value menu items and recurring promotions focused at retaining customers and attracting new ones.

Selling 101, or a Hard Knock's Manual

When communicating with a customer or prospect, you must treat this person with at least as much respect and adoration as you have for yourself. As a professional, you must keep your interactions cordial and friendly, while not getting too familiar or personal.

I know that's day one stuff for a salesperson, but we need to get back to the beginning for this. As an adult, peaceful citizen and business person, there are only a few people I will give a pass to when it comes to being professional. These are only temporary, however.

For example, do not expect children to behave respectfully if they haven't been properly taught. Rebellion is natural, but cannot be tolerated for too long. In my own case, those rebellious years helped me understand the need and benefits of acting better as a person and treating people well. If you're dealing with a rebellious kid, get them a job and keep them in school. Sports, clubs, perhaps even ROTC or the military can help your kids get discipline and structure that will serve them better in life.

Since we're going back to the beginning, I will talk about my first job. At the time, I hated it. That's very common for young people. They claim to know everything and expect the world to hand over everything they want. (I speak from experience, so no offense to anyone.)

When I turned 16, I had a small party and I can remember my family talking about that I was able to get a job. I hadn't even got my driver's license yet. I was having trouble with school grades.

I was socially awkward and dealing with (and would for years) under-treated mental health issues. My family life was in shambles. I hardly saw my dad. He was working a lot.

My mom was in her second bad marriage. I had few friends, let alone any girls that liked me. I couldn't even enjoy the moment, an important milestone for many young people, because their input just depressed me.

Sob story aside, I was a mess. The last thing on my mind was getting a job. As best as I can remember, I would have preferred looking for one at my own pace and one I actually would have wanted to do. That said, I was arrogant enough to think I was qualified for something better than what I got. I made that known on a few applications, as I recall. I was an idiot.

So having been compelled to enter the job market, I was offered a position at a local ice cream parlor, a famous company name, in fact.

I. Hated. It.

I know I said that, but it's worth repeating. Would I do this type of work again? Of course. I'm not "too good" for it. I don't want to, but if I had to, most certainly.

I don't respect anyone who thinks they are too good for a certain profession. Yes, I understand that you may have worked your way up, but never forget where you came from. If you come from money, congratulations!
You have all the more reason to show respect for the kind of people that helped your family achieve what they did. We're all in this together! (If you've never worked a "real" job, give it a try. You'll learn more than you ever expected.)

Being in high school, I could mostly work evenings and weekends. My boss, the franchise owner and operator, planned employee schedules so that at younger employees were off either Friday or Saturday night. He believed that everyone needed a social life. To be clear, I had none. I eventually did meet people that became good friends, but as one does, I preferred hanging out with them than working.

That didn't bode well. I was being inconsistent in keeping hours. I didn't want to work anyway. I wanted money, sure, but I felt I deserved more. In all the time I worked there, I was given a single raise of a whopping twenty five cents per hour. I wasn't really spending much, and I did appreciate a little more.

That was around a dollar more per day. Honestly, handling money for me was easy — as long as I controlled it. (I wasn't practicing any method. I just spent very little. Either way, in the waning days of my employment, I was given less and less hours until I was not on the schedule. I was still a minor, so my mother called the store upset. I forget how the exchange went, but it was time to find another job (also not my decision).

Generational Collisions

Actually, there is a sort phenomenon going on now regarding work ethic in young people. I've noticed it in the past couple of years especially. We have seen a massive increase of job openings and way too many companies not being fully staffed.

There are numerous reasons for this, of course. What I've noticed is that many young people are wanting more hours. They want to go to work. That makes me confident about the future of our society.

Millennials (such as myself) and Gen Z are not lazy or stupid; we just need to grow up a little. The same goes for every generation past and every generation to come.

(To my older readers: Don't kid yourself. You were just as bad or worse than I was.)

Ever heard of the Roaring Twenties? That's right, Your grandparents and great grandparents were just as wild and crazy as kids are today.

Don't be so critical of young people. Hold them accountable and they'll do fine. By the way, no matter what your age, you always have something to learn and room for growth!

Twenty years ago, a poor worker would not be employed for too long at an entry level position. Whether they were fired or quit is irrelevant. The process of termination is rarely swift. Admittedly, my first boss put up with me much longer than he should have. If I were to speak to him today, I would have a lot to apologize and thank him for.

Whether today's young people are modern employees is up to their managers and supervisors. If they do even the bare minimum, they're often good enough for the job or at least worth keeping around.

You're welcome to disagree, and I wouldn't tolerate bare minimum myself. However, with enough time and experience, they can do better, even if it means working somewhere else.

(If anyone is tolerating "bare minimum" in a workplace today, it's most likely because of their own staffing shortage.)
Losing a job because of a bad attitude, poor work ethic, attendance issues, or just walking away from one (insert your own reason for doing so here) will have a substantial impact on finding (or not being able to find) another job.

That's obvious, but how did that happen? I'm sure they have their own sob story, but that's not the point. It will, in one way or other, determine how they approach the next job.

Sadly, too many managers are more concerned with labor costs than appreciating their employees. I'm not saying those managers are bad people as much as I'm saying that an otherwise good person could be a bad manager. Without appreciation, there is only depreciation, and everything goes downhill.

"When the leader speaks, people listen." John C. Maxwell

Brief Business School, or Selling 102

It is possible to be in a management or supervisory position with no leadership skills. The functional role of a manager is to operate a business. You can be promoted to a job you're not really qualified for, and this happens frequently to well-meaning individuals simply trying to advance their career. Ambition is good if it's for honest reasons.

The problem here is that management takes a lot of heat from their superiors. I've seen people be given a better position only to later regret it, and I've also seen people glad they didn't get the promotion. Others might end up quitting.

"Better" is relative to the person, of course. If it wasn't a growth opportunity, it was a waste of time. A title and/or small raise is very tempting for some.

One thing I want to mention here is that taking a new job just for a dollar or two more per hour is rarely worth it. This is mostly referring to anyone that "job hops" and hasn't spend any significant time somewhere. If you simply want to do something else, that's fine and you're certainly welcome to do that.

Even then, be sure you're doing it for the right reasons and get all the information you can. If you want to look for a new job, make it worth the time and effort. Ask the right questions, learn everything you can about the new company, its competition, working hours and so forth.

Corporate structures are necessary for running a company. That needs to be understood. To survive and prosper in the modern business world, expansion is vital. In my last book, I said regression is better than stagnation.

Even regression means movement, and it can improve. Stagnation means you're not going anywhere, and you start to rot. I would imagine this contributes to burnout in many people.

Corporate Collision Course, or Selling 103

Anyone who thinks "corporations are evil" probably hasn't thought it through. Yes, there are numerous companies that have dirty secrets and some have done horrible things. However, all of it can be traced to at least one person mishandling their authority, miscommunication, overestimation, underestimation, or basically anything unprofessional or illegal.

This is the fault of those who did it, not the corporation itself. Many times, the guilty party (or parties) knew exactly what they were doing. It goes without saying that they had no business being in that position.

A corporation, by definition, is simply a legal entity. It was originally developed hundreds of years ago as a way to limit monetary losses on large investments such as a fleet of merchant ships traveling abroad. From a business and commerce perspective, this makes sense.

For example, a modern limited liability corporation (LLC) is designed in such a way that should the business go under, the investors (executives, owners, stakeholders, etc.) only lose their original buy in and aren't on the hook to pay more than the law requires.

A proprietorship or partnership, by comparison, are completely owned by a person or persons that have full stake in the company. These are the ones that are gone when the big box store comes to town. A corporation is in a better position to sell their assets or possibly merge.

A locally owned family business can be annihilated if they follow a traditional proprietorship structure. It only makes sense if you have no competition. Interestingly, many of them do reorganize this, and they may turn a profit if they're later bought out.

LIES. LIES. LIES!

Some people are resigned to the fact they have to work and can't do better and that's just the way it is. It's not. People succeed everyday. Maybe it's insignificant to you, and maybe you'll never hear about it, but it's true.

I *need* to work. I *want* to be paid.

Understand and believe that concept, and your career might just make a turn for the better. What does it mean? Well, have you ever wondered why anyone would keep going to a job they hate? Other than the money or planning retirement, there's a need there.

Some people think if they won a million dollars, they'd never work again and they'd simply live happily ever after. Sure, you could put the money in the bank and live off the interest (if that can even still be done), but you'll probably get bored sooner than you think. At that point, you have a few choices. Go back to work, start a business, or spend it.

If you do the last one, you know what happens. It's gone within a few years. Bad idea.
"Well you don't need a million dollars, to do nothing, man. Just take a look at my cousin, he's broke, don't do sh*t." - *Office Space*

The first one is an option, and maybe would serve most well to the aforementioned blessed individual. If you're happy living modestly, you can have all your bills paid and go on some nice vacations. Still, you go to work like normal, maybe only part time.

You'll see some people doing this during retirement. My own mother retired and I noticed right away she didn't know what to do with herself. She works part time now, but she is hesitant to do much more. She also has told me she doesn't want to make a lot of money.

"I think a person who says that would lie about other things, too." - Zig Ziglar

To her credit, she has had a few little businesses of her own. She often helps her sister during shows and events as well. My aunt is gifted with the drive and personality and my mother is gifted with a love of being around people and enjoys working with children.

I keep telling my mother to become a professional tutor or get her master's degree. I've also suggested (several times) to write a book. I'm honestly curious about stories she could tell about her life. I do believe everyone should write a book. It doesn't have to be good. It just has to be *yours*. Does that make sense? Fiction, non fiction, whatever. Make it your own!

The same goes with any creative outlet. My father is a musician and songwriter. He has a catalog of material and he's recently started writing his own books. I've mentioned to him that if he wanted to write his life story, he could change names and places to "protect the innocent", if you will. I cannot confirm whether that is good advice for everyone, but some people may find it useful.

Even if you don't win or inherit a million dollars, those are choices everyone makes to varying degrees. In any scenario, you need proper discipline with your finances, your obligations, and your business practices.
Human nature demands activity. Have you ever noticed that after awhile, some that hasn't been working (whether by choice, laid off, disability, or otherwise is irrelevant for this concept) seems to get worse?

That can be in attitude, health, socially, or a host of things combined. They sometimes develop a sense of entitlement. I would excuse elderly, accident victims and veterans from some of that, but no one else really deserves something they didn't earn.

The thing is, at some point, we are all going to feel entitled to something. If you've earned it, fine. If not, well, you need to grow up and get back to work.

The Customer Experience

I've told you about all that to make the point that each person you deal with in the business world is a real person with a real life and real stories to tell. You want their stories about you to be true, but more importantly, positive.

Let us examine a prospect named Karen (and yes, I mean *that* Karen). She wants to buy something. She has a lot going on, and this makes her feel important. Raising kids, juggling a husband (you read that right), maybe working some job (doesn't matter for this type of prospect), it's a tough life. Not to mention she's always running late, even if she's an hour early.

One day, she decides (or demands) she needs a new refrigerator. She goes to the local home improvement store and meets a friendly associate named Andy. He has been there about three years now and is the go-to guy when a customer needs appliances. He's in college right now studying engineering, and is currently training in appliance repair.

Karen sees another clueless kid and is already irritated frustrated she had to walk this far. "Why aren't refrigerators displayed outside?" She asks.

At this point, Andy actually is clueless, but he doesn't miss a beat.

"They're right over here, ma'am, and our finest brand is on special right now!"

He shows her a state-of-the-art model that has all the features: a visual display, freezer light, and for some reason a baby monitor option. She's unimpressed.

"You're selling this way too high!"

"Ma'am we have a variety of options," Andy responds. "I'm happy to show you some other excellent models within your price range."

"No, this is the exact one I need, and I must have it at least three hundred dollars lower. I also require that payment plan."

Karen points at a sign.

"I can't do anything about the price, ma'am, and that installment program is only available for another brand. I can speak with my manager about adjusting payment options for this model if you'd like."

"Please."

Before any of us get more disgusted, we can assume the worst here. She complains as high up as possible and management won't budge (by policy they can't, and legally, they don't have to). She storms out angrily (possibly loudly and spewing hateful comments) and goes to the competitor across town.

It goes much the same if not worse, and she ends up buying something at the price she wanted, even though it was not as nice as the one Andy showed her. She goes home and brags about getting the best price, telling her husband he should "trust her" with major purchases in the future because she "knows where the deals are".

Andy and his coworkers are glad to be rid of her. He's actually commended for how he handled the situation. The competitors gave the best discount they could, but Karen still wasn't satisfied, apparently. She did end up buying, however. They appreciated the sale, but they cringe at the thought she might come back one day.

So who's the winner here? Well, in a way, all three. Andy wins because he was willing to deal with one of the worst possible situations for a salesperson and he learned from it. When you face adversity, it's worth it. Even a loss can turn into a win later. It's a lot less painful to take the hit than to keep trying to avoid it.

Remember, your prospects, customers and clients can't hurt you. They're just regular people going about their lives. Anyone who would harm anyone simply trying to sell them something is truly disturbed. Don't be pushy and just move on if they're not interested.

There are numerous closing techniques you can learn, but it is possible to go too far. (I discussed high pressure earlier, but in this context I am referring to overselling and harassment.)
The competitor made a sale. It's a win, but their profit on the sale was lower than it could have been. By all means, you should get the best price, but Karen went about it all wrong. She will be given as little attention as possible in the future. They may even plan to discount anything she buys just to get rid of her. They're taking multiple losses doing this, even if they are getting her business.

However, she's not the only person doing this. If this is happening too often, and it does in many companies, you'll see higher turnover, poor morale, and fewer customers, at least satisfied ones. Of course, these losses add up and they have people working double shifts, cutting hours of others, under- or overestimation on truck orders, and then we get into logistical problems that have their own complexity.

From Prospect to Customer to Client

How did Karen win? She went to the first store and she knew already where the refrigerators were displayed. They're never outside. She perhaps thought it would be a good idea to have them outside, because more people would see them. That could have been a great suggestion to make if she had been polite about it. She could be an asset to the company, but she believes she's too good for that.

Her bias is confirmed when a handsome young man half her age is supervising the appliance department. He couldn't possibly know about how the world works and she does, and they hired him! Do they think she's not good enough for this place? She makes her disapproval known by cruelty directed toward an innocent stranger.

However, she still plans to get a refrigerator and she won't leave without one. They owe her if a woman like her isn't welcome here, she thinks. She doesn't fool anyone there, but she feels a certain power acting this way. She finally gives up, having made her "point", and finally buys at the competitor's store.

When her husband looks at it, he likes it, but he notices it's not much different from their old one. It's nice, but there wasn't anything more special than the old one. It's as if Karen knew what she wanted before she left home that day. She may have walked in the first store simply to look at prices and didn't intend to buy anything because it might be cheaper elsewhere.

Her ego didn't allow her to accept what was available there. She liked the refrigerator, but it was too expensive. Had she simply let Andy show her other options, she might have found something better than what she got for around the same price.

Karen might be an extreme example, but customers do think this way. Other than simply checking out prices and planning, not many people go into a store "just looking" anymore. Online shopping has made it unnecessary, and most people are aware many products and services can be found there at lower prices.

That means that anyone who walks into any sort of for-profit business actually *wants* to buy something. Maybe they won't. Maybe they don't have the money, and that's understandable. The fact is they want to buy something whether or not they can. Otherwise, they wouldn't have walked in.

We need to break down terms here. Until a buyer actually buys something, they are a prospect. Like prospecting for gold, they're out there looking for something. In fact, it's not an exaggeration to say that everyone in the world that hasn't bought from you yet is a prospect.

A customer is a buyer at the retail level. Whether it's a hot dog or a Mercedes, this is where the action happens. If you're in retail sales, you need to understand that these people are customers at many places (same as you) and are prospects to many more (also like you).

In general, retail customers purchasing tangible items have few requirements for what they buy. There are significant differences in customer needs versus business-to-business (B2B). Products and services offered businesses sometimes have higher prices or will be calculated based on the size of the order.

A client is a buyer of services. If you're a hairdresser, attorney, life coach, or contractor, you have clients. If your business offers any type of paid service, you have clients. If you're working a retail position (including work like serving tables and bartending), it's likely you have repeat customers. I believe repeat customers aren't just there for your products. You are actually providing a service to them. Often, your mere presence makes them happy.

These are the people that seek you out if they have questions. They respect you because they believe you know what you're doing and know how to do it. Treat these people like clients, and they'll keep coming back. Every single customer or client quite literally pays your wages. Without them, no business can succeed.

Creating Bad Customers

It's very unfortunate that many companies don't offer practical customer service and sales training for employees. Some argue that it's the responsibility of the individual to obtain their own training. I agree to an extent, because I have done it myself (and if you're reading this, so have you!).

However, this belief is careless if you expect your employees to perform well. Sure, you probably have a basic training program showing them how to do the job, but how do they fare when dealing with patrons?

If you were to hire me as a consultant, my first act would be to go into your business acting as a customer or client. Ideally, only a few people would know about a consultant being there and fewer would know it's me. I act courteous and am a model customer/client.

I probably take my time and look at your sales floor or public area. I'll be speaking with your employees about random things, picking up on things they might be afraid to tell you. I'll speak with a few customers as well. I observe things. I see just how helpful you and your staff are.

Think of me as a reverse-sales guide. Why don't people buy? Why do you have poor reviews? Why is there a negative rumor going around town because of a single incident years ago? If you're dealing with anything like that, you are (usually) the problem. Don't play the blame game. No one wins that.

People typically leave poor reviews when they're upset about something, so don't take them all at face value. Sometimes, you just can't please someone or maybe they're just a negative person. Remember, those are the customers and clients you can afford to lose.

If they keep coming back, you could be setting yourself up for failure. Why enable this sort of thing? Some people will do things simply because no one ever told them not to.
If you end up being the person that does, give them a reason why. Very few people know how to do this properly. Ideally, critique should be given in private. No one likes to be embarrassed or criticized in front of others.

If a problem arises and you can't take it aside, you aren't required to take abuse in any form or anywhere. You can walk away, escalate to proper authorities, or just keep calm and wait for them to embarrass themselves.

Years ago, I heard that a customer with a bad experience will tell up to ten more people about it. With online reviews, that number has increased. However, positive reviews are more visible and available than ever before. If you are doing something right, keep at it! The more you care and take pride in your work, the more the public will notice.

We run into a different problem here. On the surface, you could have the best company in the world. People come in and you serve them well. You give them what they want, they buy, they leave, they come back.

Wonderful! What's the problem, you ask? Your employee morale. You may be limited in how much you can pay your employees, but there is no limit to general appreciation for them, and you must communicate that. Even if they're doing bare minimum, greet them, thank them for coming to work, and ask them how they're doing. And actually listen.

I know what I said before about the bare minimum, but consider something. A lazy person probably doesn't doesn't feel appreciated. A hard worker may not be as concerned about that, but they most certainly deserve recognition. As human beings, we all want that. Your employees are just as (if not more so) important as customers and clients.

Why? You depend on them. You can have all the buyers in the world, but if your employees feel unappreciated, undervalued or overlooked, you are in a terrible position. This is when people walk away from jobs (sometimes for less pay, even), quality drops and your previously satisfied guests disappear. Worse things can happen, but let's continue.

If you're in management, you're to blame. Not the employee. The individual can only be disciplined according to their own behavior, but I would argue anything requiring formal discipline probably could have been avoided.

Some people are socially awkward and as such, they can find themselves in situations that others may have handled properly. They aren't bad people, necessarily, but it is possible that person didn't know any better.

Creating Buyers

One of the most insulting things in the world is for people to assume you already know something that you were never told. Don't take your own knowledge and experience for granted to the point you think everyone else has it. Just as important, don't look down on anyone for not knowing something. You were there at some point, and probably will be again.

Any sort of negative judgment against said person is just broadcasting your own ignorance. You lose respect and credibility. You trained that person for a job, and they're capable, but they're lacking something. Even a socially adept person needs a level of guidance for dealing with the public.

This is why I think that not training sales people is careless. The designated salesperson keeps at least nine others employed. So it can be said that around ten percent of employees at a given company make money for the remaining ninety percent. In today's workplace, a "sales associate" is not necessarily doing only sales.

That job title may sound more professional, but the average "sales associate" doesn't really know how to sell. They spend time stocking, cleaning and scanning. While all of that needs to be done, employees can be taught how to sell more. In reality, everything is sales, even if you're collecting trash.

If you want to improve your customer service and sales skills, all of it has to do with people skills.

"It's all about rapport." - Jordan Belfort

If your only motivation is for the paycheck, you're just asking for trouble in the long run. You attitude suffers and it spreads. It's fine if you want to make more money, but it starts with the right attitude. You can't create positive changes if you won't change yourself.

"Stop thinking in reverse!" - Jonathan Baltzly

Let's say you've been gifted with the best employees in the world. Your team is top notch, and you know they're capable of great things. You picked them out yourself. You've even sold them on why their job is important and how it helps people.

They do what they're told and they respect you. You're doing it for the right reasons, but you notice a problem. Your sales are in the tank. You're of the opinion that your time is valuable. It is, but everyone gets only twenty four hours a day, and every moment is precious.

Did you forget that? You can't put yourself on such a high pedestal that you forget where you came from. Anyone that does that is a fool and isn't worthy of success.

True Story

The previously described team is based on something I experienced a few years ago. I will not name anyone, because I am not innocent in this matter. With that said, here's my story.

I was seeking a life coach and there was one locally I checked out because his company had a formal training program on site. It was way outside of my budget. I knew that going in. In my mind, I wanted to talk to the coach and discuss any options for someone in my position. I was willing to volunteer (in other words "negotiate') my time to help out in exchange for a little coaching until I was able to pay what they were asking.

When I walked in, I didn't see the coach anywhere. I saw a room full of tables, chairs, computers, a coffee pot and some refreshments, and to my right was a bookshelf of numerous titles the coach had written. No prices were listed (keep that in mind). I was soon greeted by an attractive young woman who led me to a table and had me fill out their questionnaire.

So far, so good. It was mostly about my goals and dreams and asked how they could help. She had several things to do, so she was going back and forth between talking to me and handling other tasks.

I would have been fine with that, except her job was sales. I really didn't know how to take her because she wasn't with me the entire time. For about an hour or more, only one other person (one of their clients, in fact) spoke to me aside from her and another lady at the door.

I honestly felt unheard and was getting pretty frustrated. They were friendly, of course, and the gentleman that spoke to me during the break mentioned he hated seeing anyone sitting alone. I was pretty impressed, actually. That's a client you want!

So, the very motivated young woman finally came back to the table again (this was probably the fourth time she sat down and talked me). Each time, I was simply talking about this and that (on topic, of course, but I don't remember any specifics).

I counted at least three times throughout the series the conversations where she interrupted me, literally mid-sentence. When I called her on this, she denied it, rolled her eyes and gave some lame excuse saying she was doing something else and it wasn't interrupting.

"Excuses are useless. The only one you'll ever need is if you bump into somebody." - Jonathan Baltzly

Irritation and resentment brewing already, I was ready to corner the coach after he finished his presentation. I simply wanted a few minutes to talk and maybe work out some arrangement. At the time, I was single, and I did not feel comfortable telling an attractive young woman that I couldn't afford it.

I believed they'd stop talking to me or look down on me or write me off as a "waste of time". No one that wants to buy is a waste of your time. Maybe they can't afford it, and you move on, but you better respect them as a person!

This is the point where you can really impress a customer. If you can't help them, find someone who can, and they will appreciate it. This is time invested, not wasted, and it does pay off. Who do you think they'll come back to later?

Getting back to the story, I don't know whether or not they would have stopped talking to me. There were different options at various prices, but she seemed only concerned in selling a coaching program. There was also a retreat they were hosting soon.

While talking to me, she mentioned several times that sales required a "thick skin". I knew that. That's why I was there. I needed help in that department.

Why she felt the need to repeat it, I don't know. Maybe she was reminding herself of that because I was being difficult. (This sort of rhetoric can imply you don't believe what you're saying or that you're not what you claim.) This capable young woman with a lot of potential was not prepared to deal with me.

Sometime early in our interactions, she told me that I kept putting up a wall. I didn't realize it, and I was genuinely surprised. I think it was just not wanting to admit I didn't have the money. Again, that was the entire reason I was there. I had to figure that stuff out.

At the end of the event, attendees lined up to meet the coach. I am the last person in line (as best as I recall). She is nearby and mentions that I should go to the retreat with maybe two people left in front of me. I don't remember what I responded exactly, but she answered.

"You'll make your money back." (Like it was nothing.)

"You can't guarantee that." (I'm sure he heard all this.)

"You can!" (What was that supposed to mean?)

If I was frustrated before, I was furious now. That was insulting to me, but to be fair, she hadn't been told anything about my financial situation. I'm ready to spill everything to this guy and convince him I deserve a chance. However, I didn't expect what happened next. As soon as I was in front of this man, I knew he was a person I would never lie to. I wasn't lying about anything, but I was hiding something. Right then, that wall came crashing down. That day, he had been speaking about people that were living at level two and not going after level ten opportunities. It was a wonderful presentation, and I did enjoy listening to him speak.

"Are you at level two instead of going for level ten?" He asked, kindly and sincerely.

"I'm a level ten person in a level one world," I answered. That is exactly what I said, and for some reason, at least at that moment, I believed it.

"I understand," he responded.

I wanted to say "Do you? The people that need your help the most don't have what you're asking. You can't possibly have forgotten where you came from."

Instead, I go on some rant about my bills and other things that weren't anyone's concern but mine. It was probably very brief, but he did hear me out.

"So it really is the money for you," he said.

I was speechless. The entire time, I was convinced he was concerned only about money or else this would be more affordable.

I said something about the YouTube comments not being monitored, and he admitted they hadn't been.

"I'll do that," I said. "And I'll show up before you, leave late, whatever you need."

And I meant it. I was willing to sacrifice my time, pay for the gas to get there (it was about half an hour from my home), and work long hours when I wasn't at my job basically for free, simply because I knew I needed help they offered.

He sort of nodded and said, "We'll see what we can do for you. God bless you."

Then he turned away. I'm somehow compelled to move toward the exit. I wasn't told to leave, mind you. They had coordinated in such a way that people feel the need to leave.

That's not a joke, either. The staff moved to different places, changed their postures, and basically turned their backs on me. I may have tried stay if I had recognized it at the time.

My best guess is that it was a security procedure, but I've only considered that in retrospect. There was a strong psychological aspect to it. One that made me very uncomfortable. I may have deserved that, or maybe not. Maybe it was nothing personal, or maybe it was. I will never know the reason for it. Perhaps the strangest part about that is how quickly it happened, as in only a few seconds.

"I've learned that people will forget what you said, people will forget what you did, but people will never forget how you made them feel." - Maya Angelou

As I was about to leave, I asked how much the books were. She answered, almost disinterested. I left hopeful, because maybe they could work something out. A day or two later, a gentleman called and I admitted to him that I was probably too hard on that young woman. He laughed. I have no idea what was said about me after I left. I don't really want to, and I don't care anyway.

I asked if I joined the online course (the lowest priced package offered) if I could attend live events. I was local and would have definitely been able to show up a couple times a month. He said it wasn't possible, because they kept that room very secure for "obvious reasons". I didn't know what he meant.

I wanted to say, "I don't follow." I didn't say that, but we eventually end the call cordially and I said I'd think about it. I deduced that it was out of my price range, so I ordered a book from their website. A day or two later, another man calls me and asks how it's going for me.

"I haven't received it yet," I answered.

From there, it sounded pretty sloppy on his end. How do you make the mistake of confusing a digital product from a tangible product? I bought a physical copy. Somewhere in our conversation, coaching options were mentioned. I told him an amount I could wrap my head around. Click.

He hung up on me! I will admit, the amount I gave was completely unfair. I understand that now. I'm not really a cheapskate and didn't plan on paying the least possible for long. That was the point.

If they helped me get to a position where I could pay more, I would happily reimburse them and become an example of what they claimed they could do for a client. It goes without saying that if I could do it over, I would have handled it differently.

I did receive the book eventually. It looked like it had been poorly packaged and there were numerous errors in it. Regardless, I ordered another, and for what it's worth, the coach had signed that one with a personalized message. I had a lot to learn, and I hope they learned some things, too.

Moving On

Would I work with that coach in the future? I don't know. If I do, it will only be if I am able to pay him. The same goes for anything, and you need to realize that.

"The laborer is worthy of his hire." - Jesus Christ

No one wants to work for free. Even someone who volunteers is in it for the positive feeling they get. I respect anyone who volunteers for a worthy cause. However, this is the full verse.

"And in the same house remain, eating and drinking such things as they give: for the labourer is worthy of his hire. Go not from house to house." - Luke 10:7

Within context, the disciples are being told that when they're out ministering, they are to accept what is offered. They're told to operate from one location. If they weren't welcome in the town they visited, they simply left.

I don't think that means not to sell door to door, but the point is that there is work to be done, and needs must be met. They aren't working for free, nor should anyone unless they just want to.

I was honestly willing to volunteer. If you're ever in a position where you can help someone in a significant way and they're willing to work for it. Give them a chance. People like that are rare. Listen to them and discuss what can be done.

There's that old (especially stupid and useless) excuse: "If we do it for you, we would have to do it for everyone."

LIE!

No you don't, and I can prove it. What's such-and-such paying? You can't tell me? Exactly! I don't want to know. It's also not such-and-such's concern what I'm paying. Period. Don't block someone's success. You're better than that. It's not a hand out or showing favoritism if someone actually intends to earn it.

Listening to that person is time well spent, not wasted. Remember, anyone that hasn't bought is a prospect. That one person you go the extra mile for might make all the difference in the world.

Now, as am a realist and business person, I don't suggest that this become so common that no one makes a profit. No. Far from it. You'll be able to spot the fakes very quickly. If they're performing well, however, you made the right call. You both have a bright future!

Maybe you're not in such a position, but how you treat others is a reflection of what you think of yourself. A person that seems to have it together usually doesn't. We all know someone with an ego the size of the moon. (If you don't, you might be that person.)

If they're acting high and mighty and treat others as if they're beneath them, that tells you they hate themselves. They'll deny it, but in reality, they have no reason to behave differently because their internal monologue says "I'm worthless and so is everyone else."

People of all ages and every profession think like that, and it's very sad. We all matter and we all want to be heard. Whether its an employee, coworker, customer, client, prospect, clergy, real estate agent, mechanic, Ken or Karen, we're all the same. We breathe the same air, we eat, sleep, and go to the bathroom.

So in work and life, remember what Brother Jonathan told you. You have a real person in front of you. In a professional setting, courtesy and kindness go a long way. The lack thereof will lead nowhere good.

If your type of business allows it, remain seated when closing a sale or negotiating a deal. If you're standing and the buyer is seated, hold a posture that is genuine and welcoming.

If you're seated, and they are standing, either rise to greet them or offer them a seat. I recommend practicing improving your body language, because repeated use will make it feel more natural. If you only learn a few tips and make them habits you will be amazed how you start feeling! I learned that doing it myself, and it was a game changer.

Also, your vocal tone makes a huge impact. As the saying goes, "it's not what you say, it's how you say it". That includes your intention, choice of words, tone of voice, your attitude and so on. Record yourself talking as if you're at work, and listen carefully.

Be conscious of how you're talking to people, and be mindful of the conversations you have. I make these suggestions because I practice them myself. If they work for me, they can work for anyone.

You may not be like me, but I truly want to help people. There are people you care about, and I have no doubt you want to see them succeed in life. Take some time to consider how you show up for people.

How are you seen by others? It really doesn't matter until you think of yourself as person worthy of success and happiness and act accordingly.

Don't be motivated by what others think of you, though. People will either like you or not, and that's OK. If you're improving and growing, you will inspire others to as well. Setting a good example is one of the best things a person can do for others.

Do you feel like you're inadequate? That's a lie. Act as if you're more than enough. Don't talk about it or tell anyone what you're tying to accomplish, just act that way (i.e. act as if you're already where you want to be). Talk is cheap. Don't talk a big game, start playing it!

I hope you have found this information helpful. Writing this has been a pleasure and a privilege. There are many more stories to tell, but those will have to wait. Thank you so much for reading. Hopefully, I'll be reading your book soon!

Until next time, this has been your brother in the game of life,

Jonathan Baltzly

Also by Jonathan Baltzly

Beyond Normality

Stop Thinking in Reverse

Made in the USA
Columbia, SC
22 February 2023